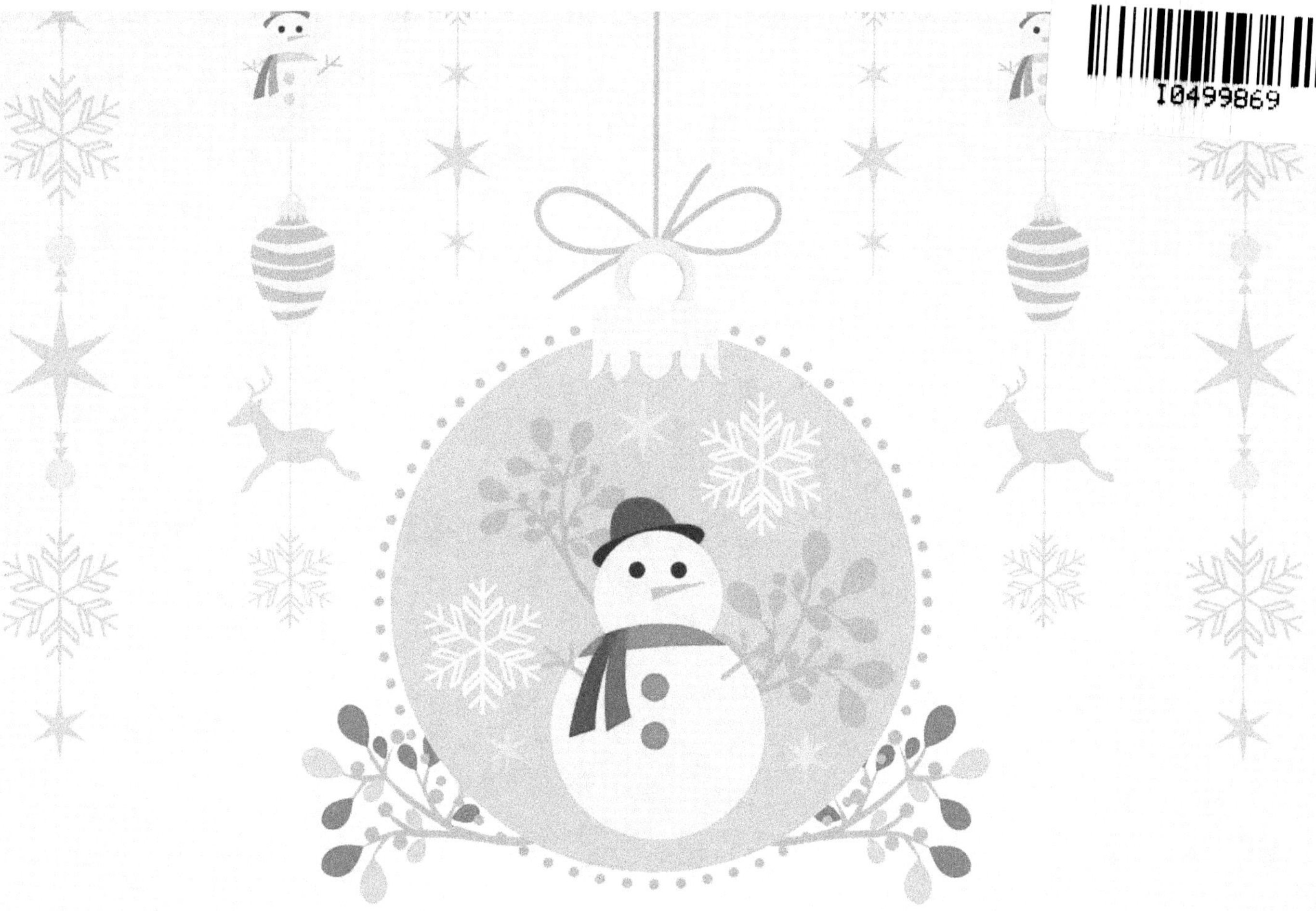

# Merry
# CHRISTMAS

## This Books Belongs To

..............................................................

..............................................................

..............................................................

..............................................................

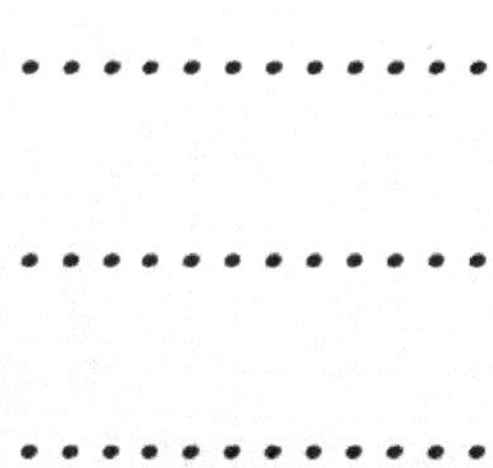

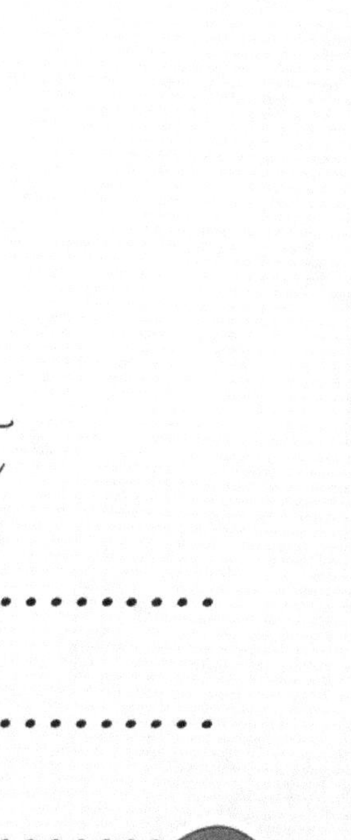

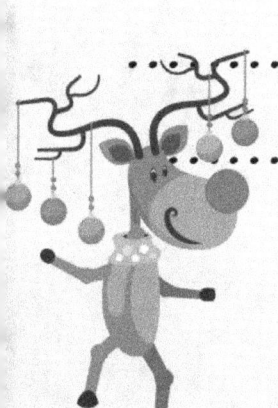

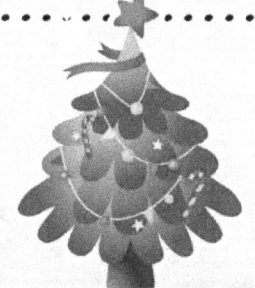

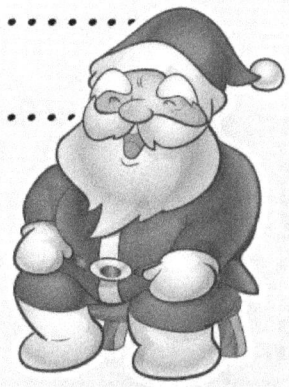

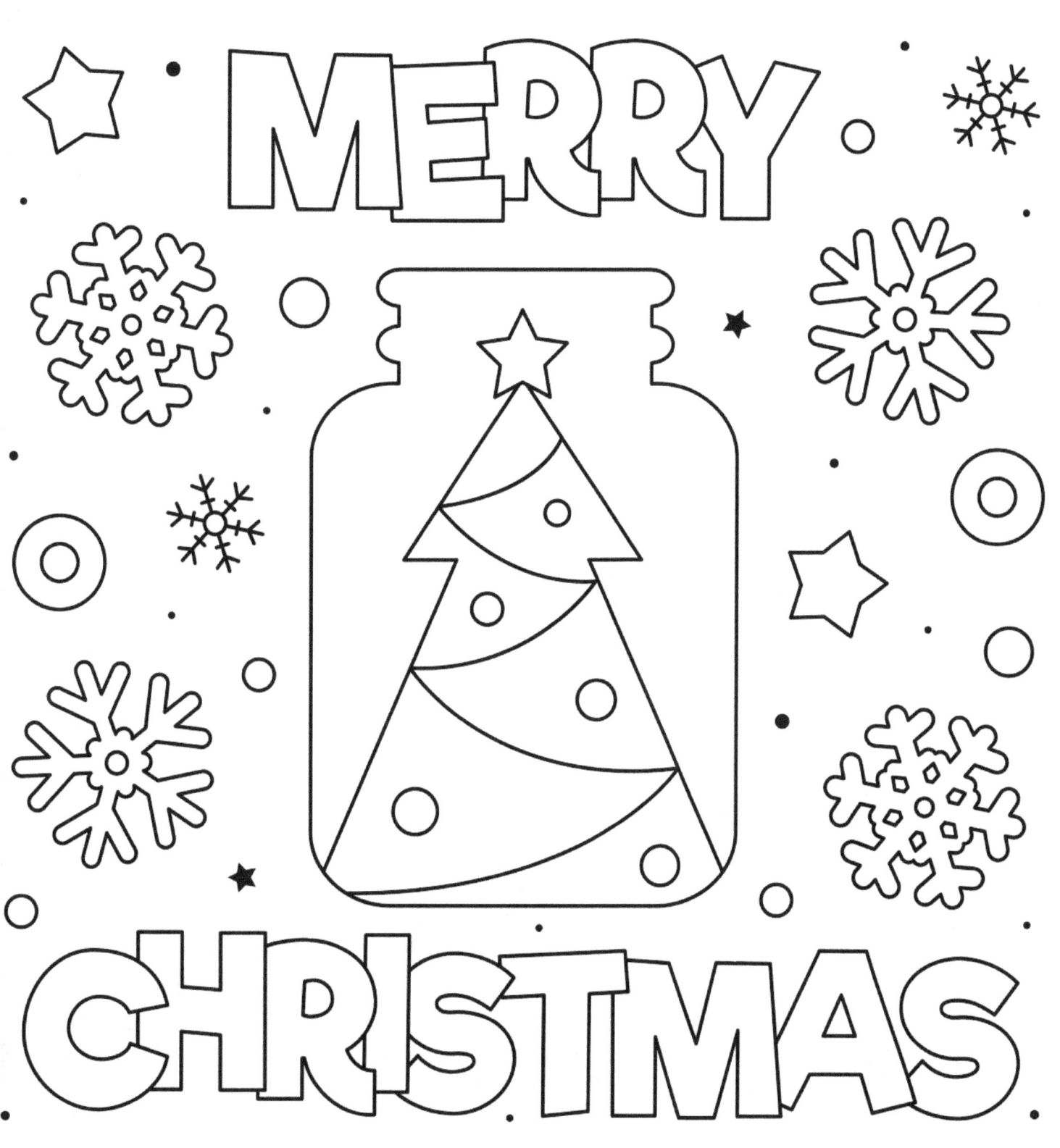

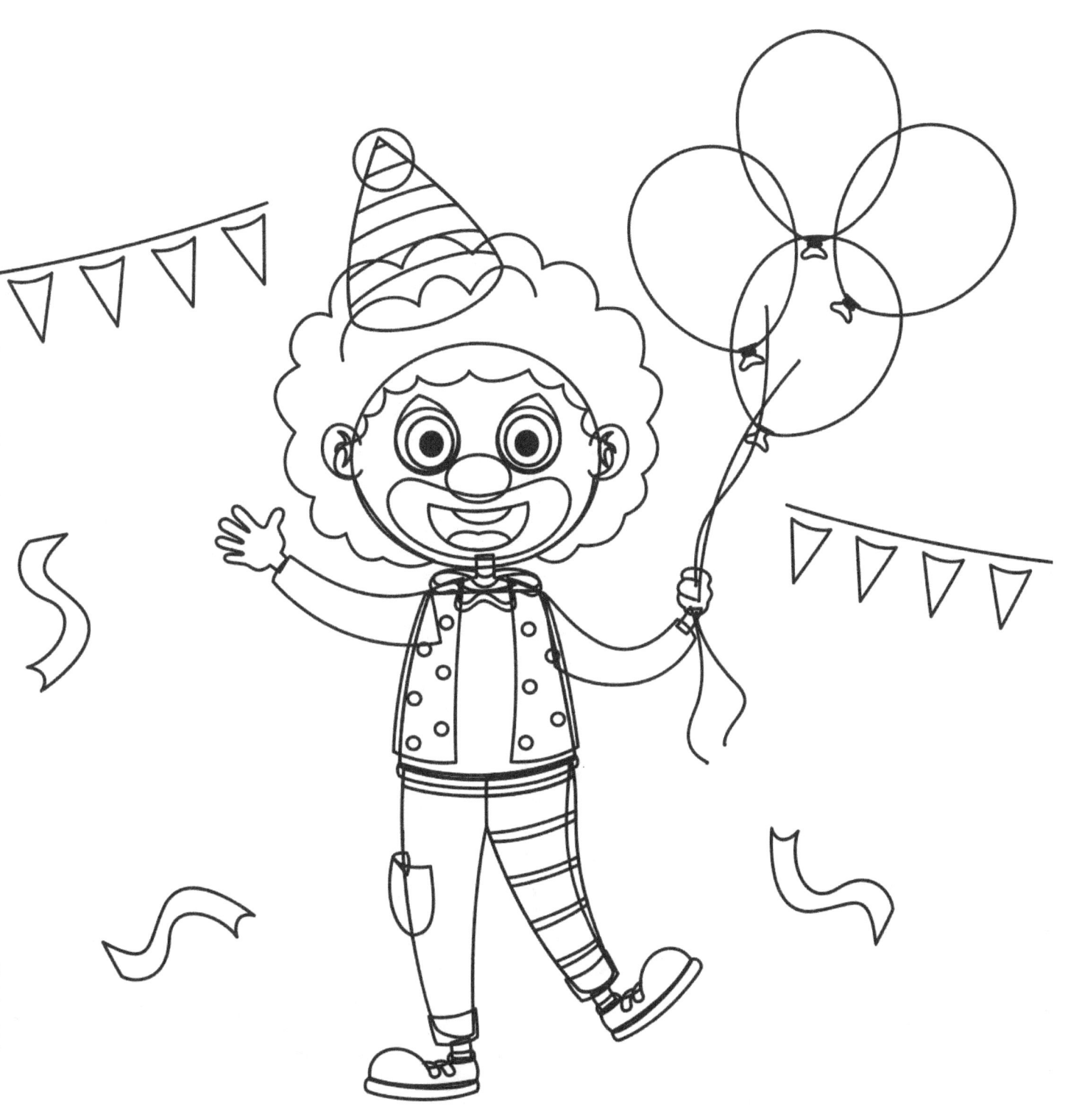

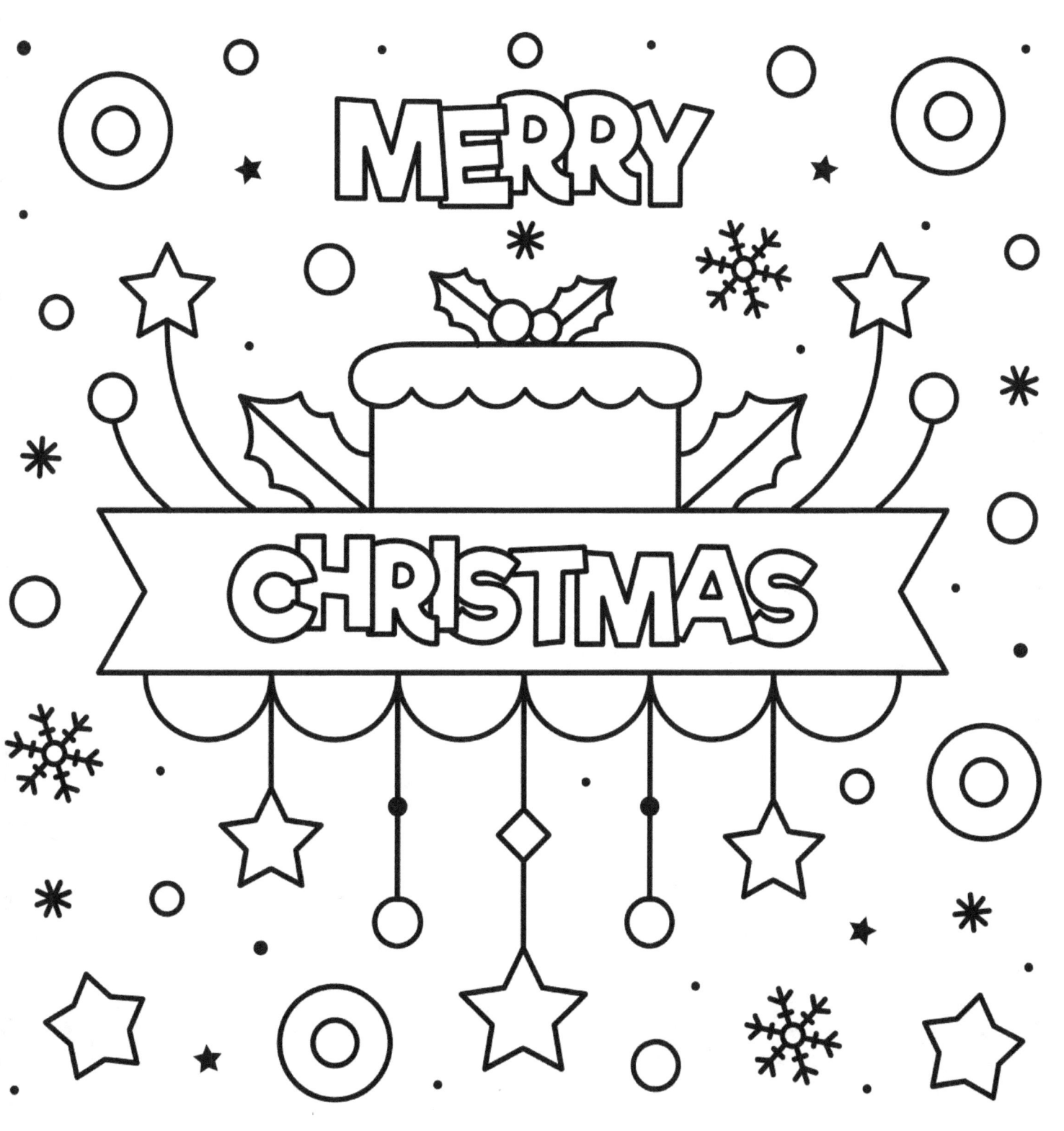

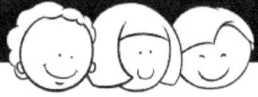

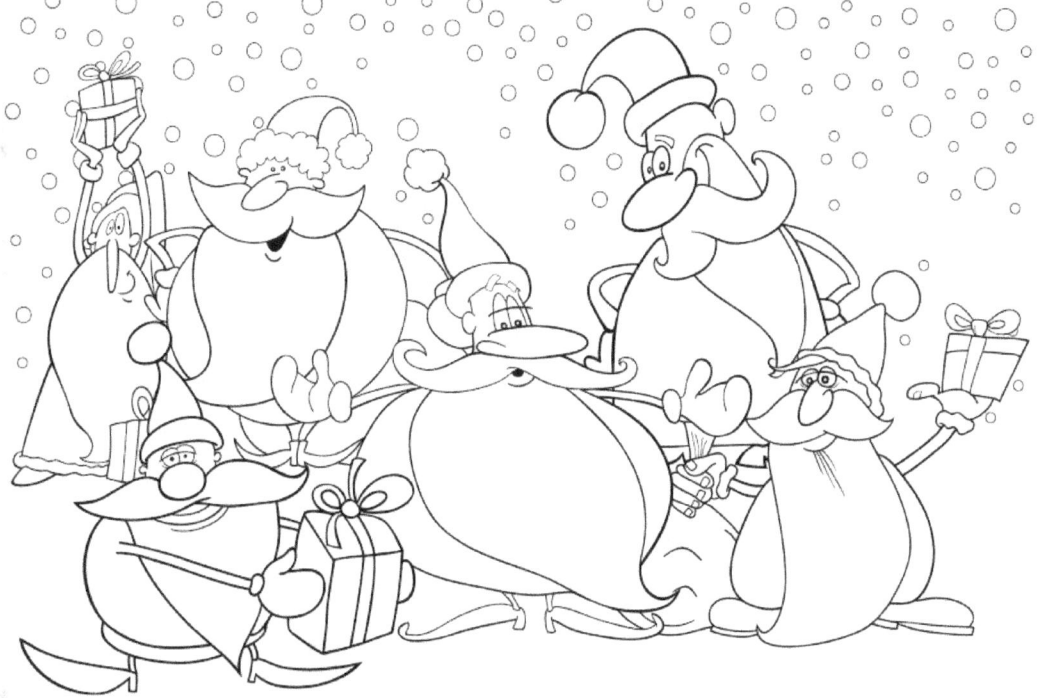

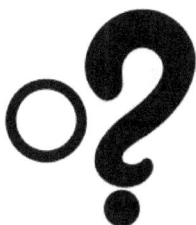

FIND
**7**
DIFFERENCES

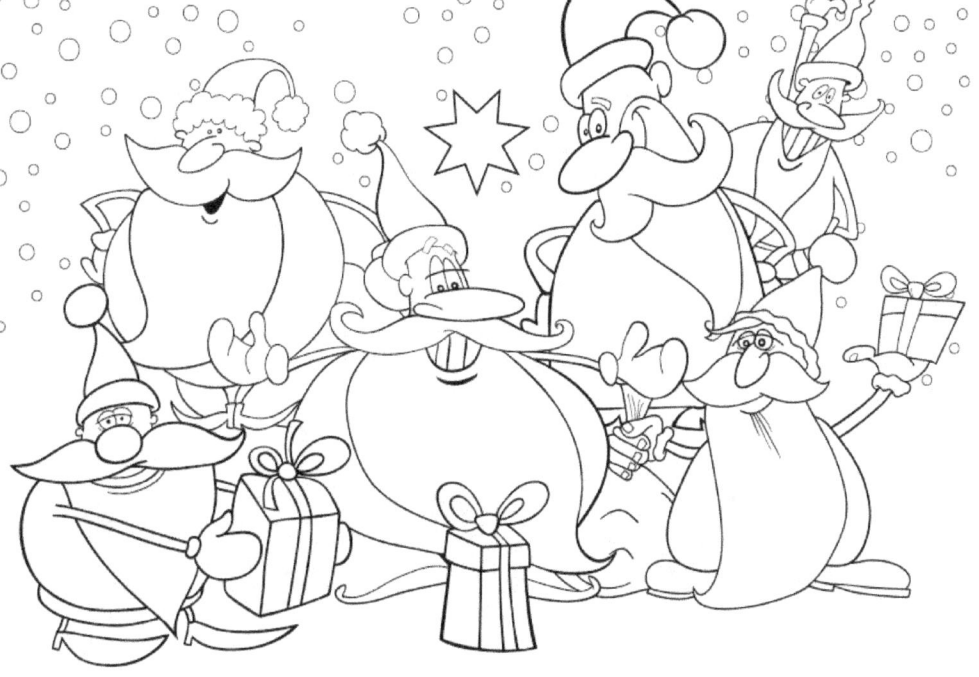

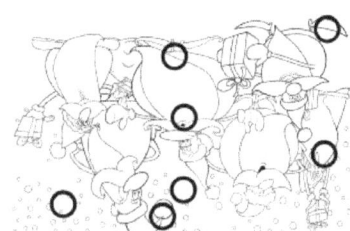

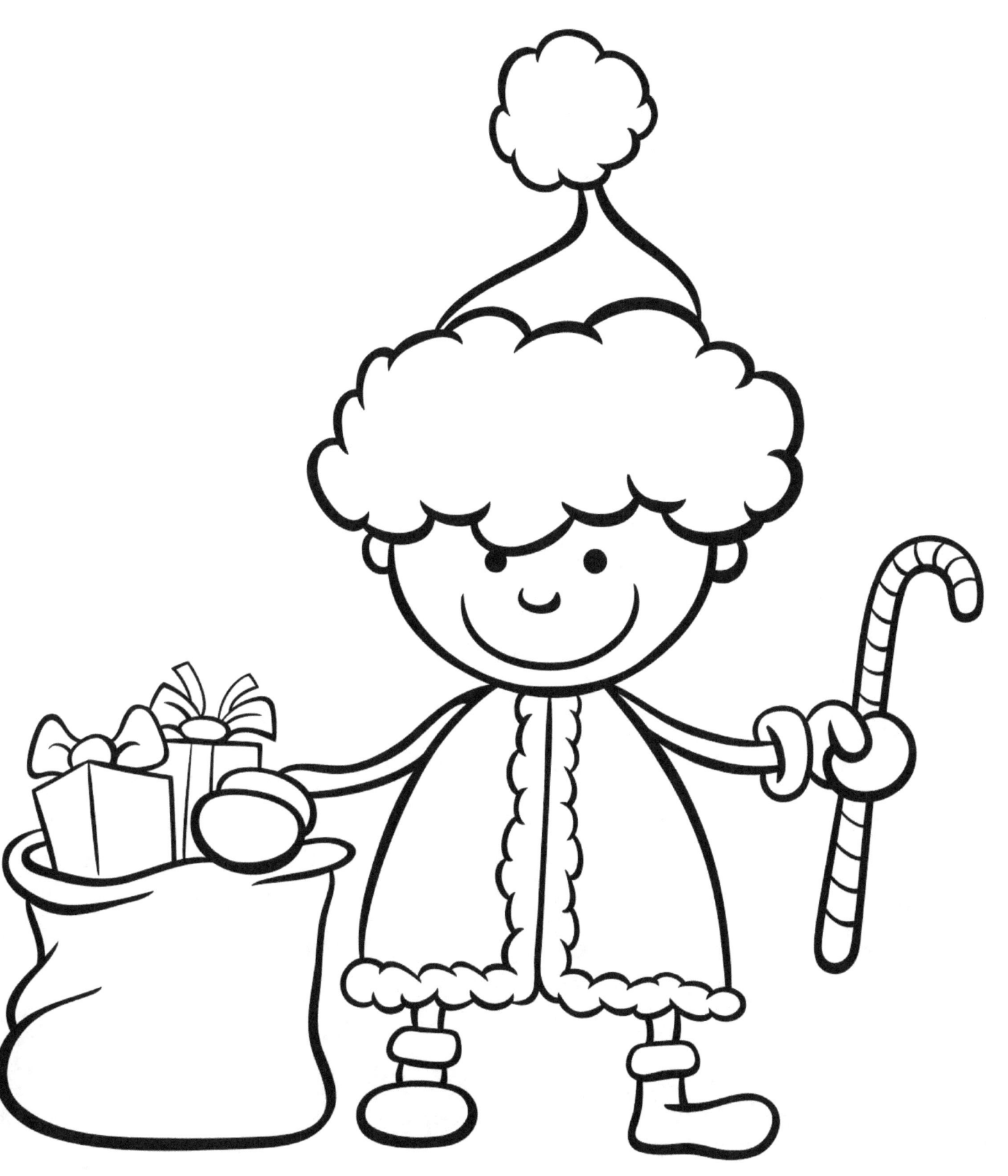

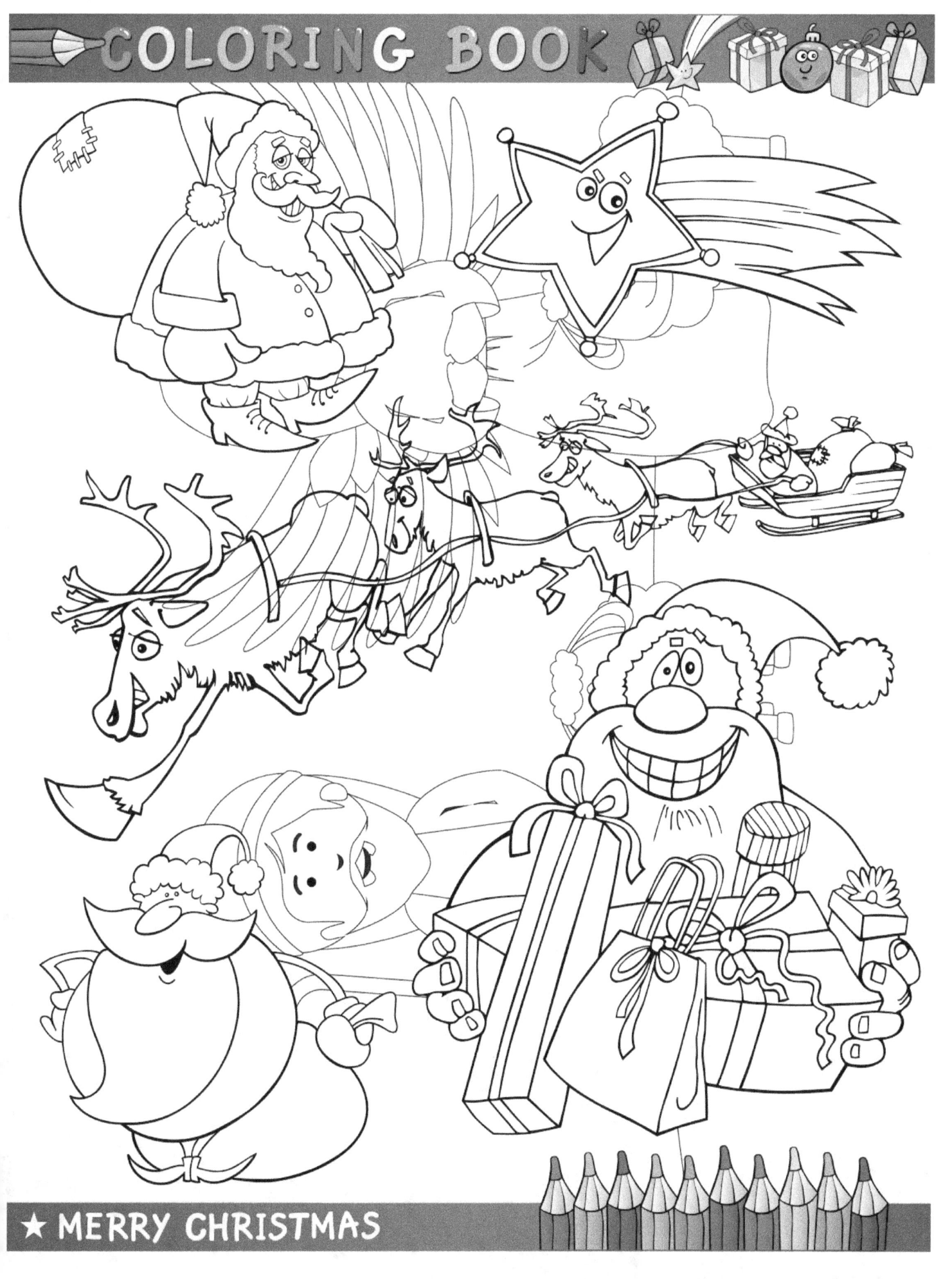

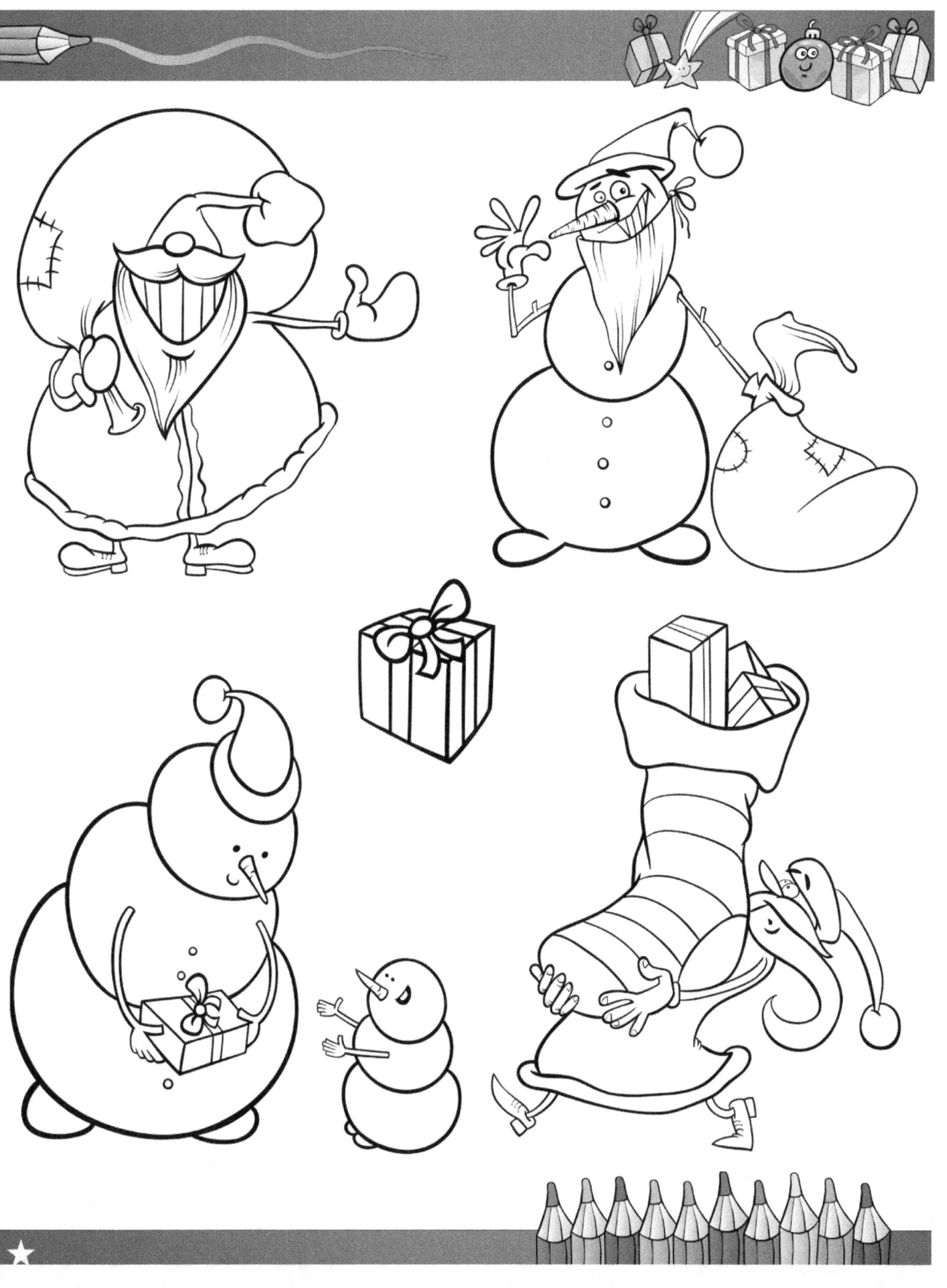

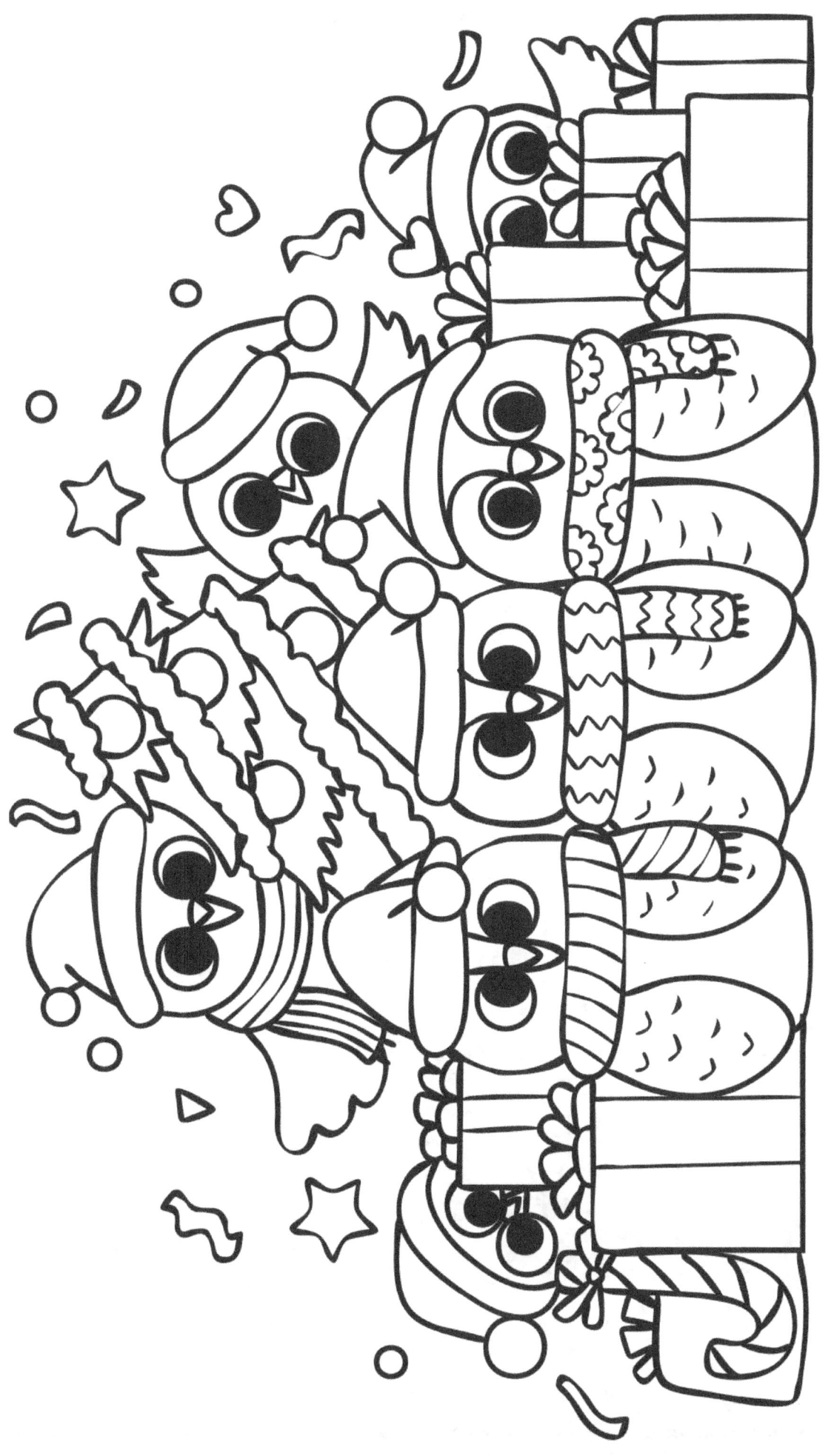

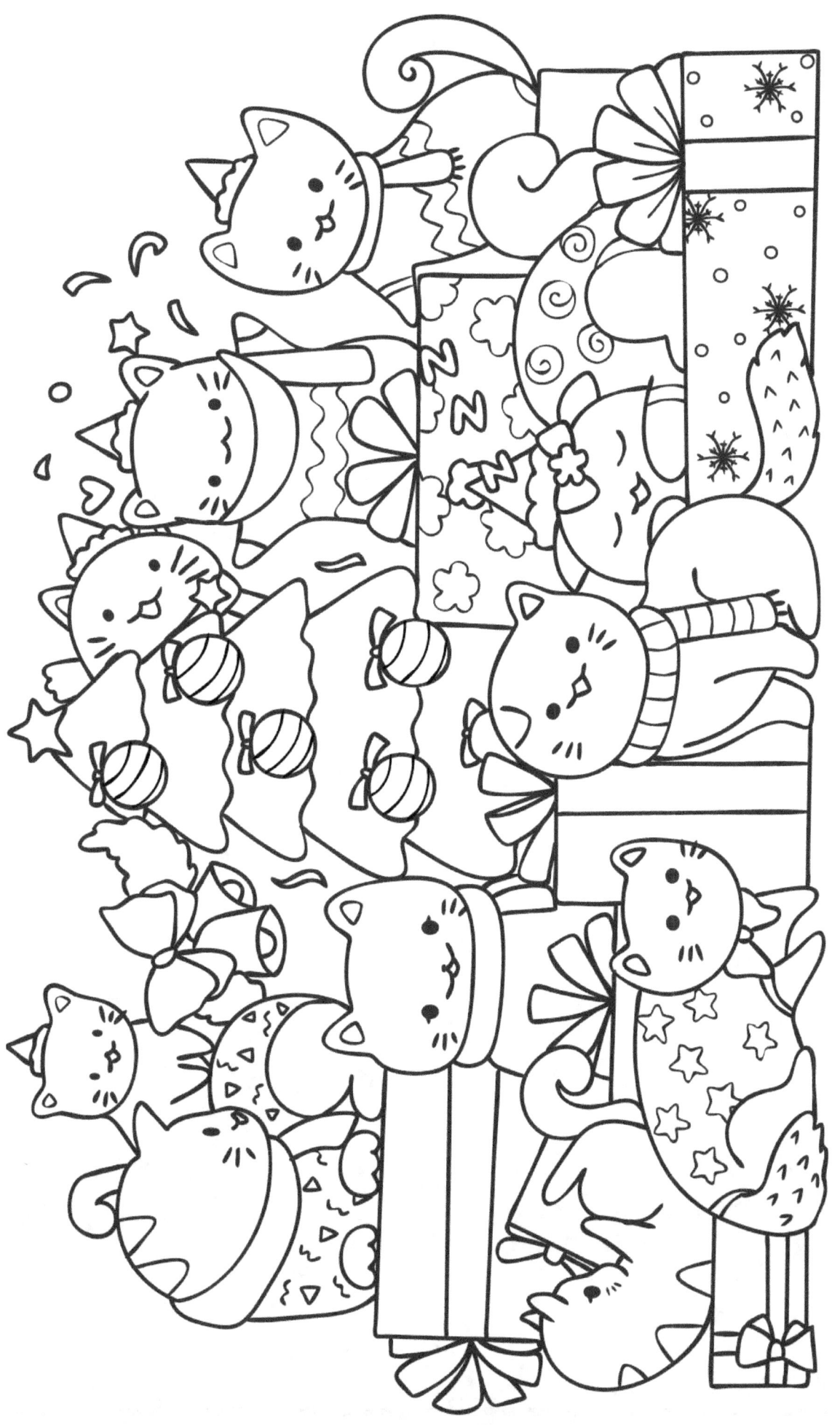

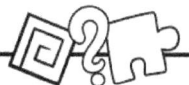

CHRISTMAS

FIND
ONE
OF A KIND

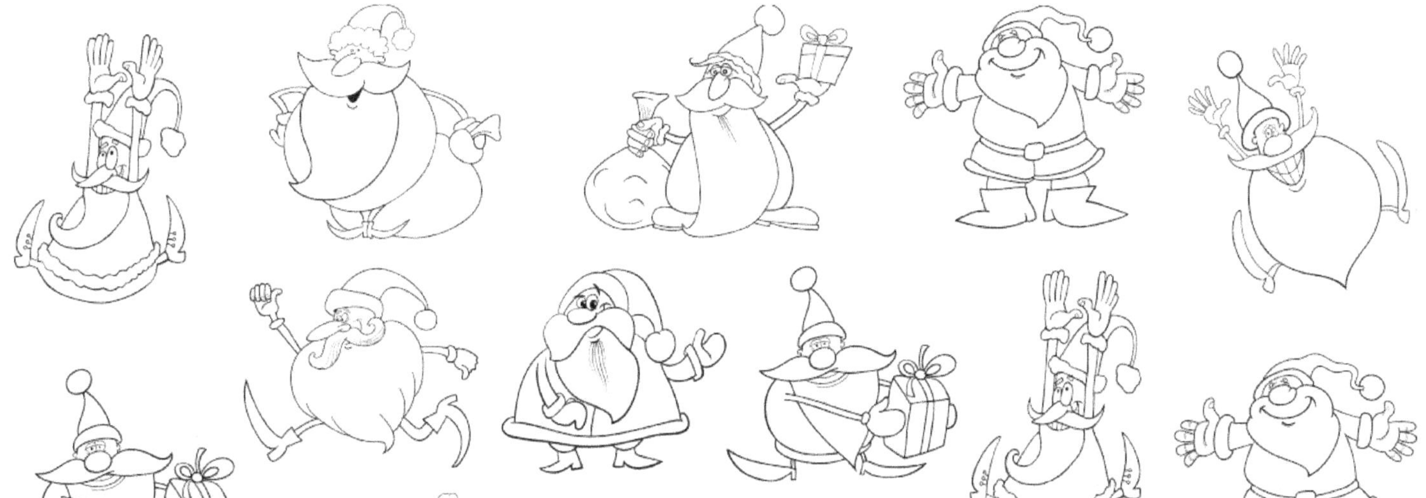

ANSWER

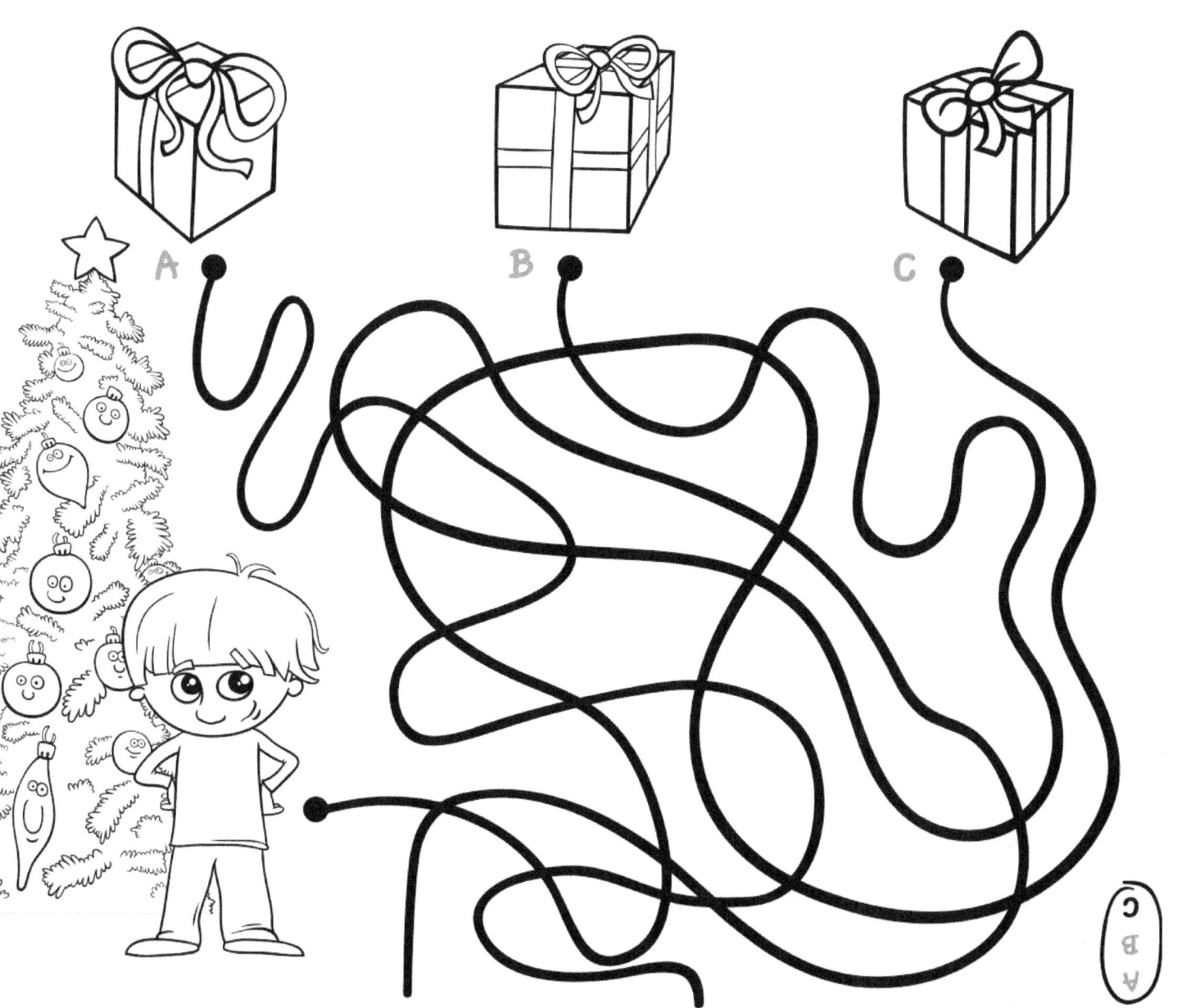

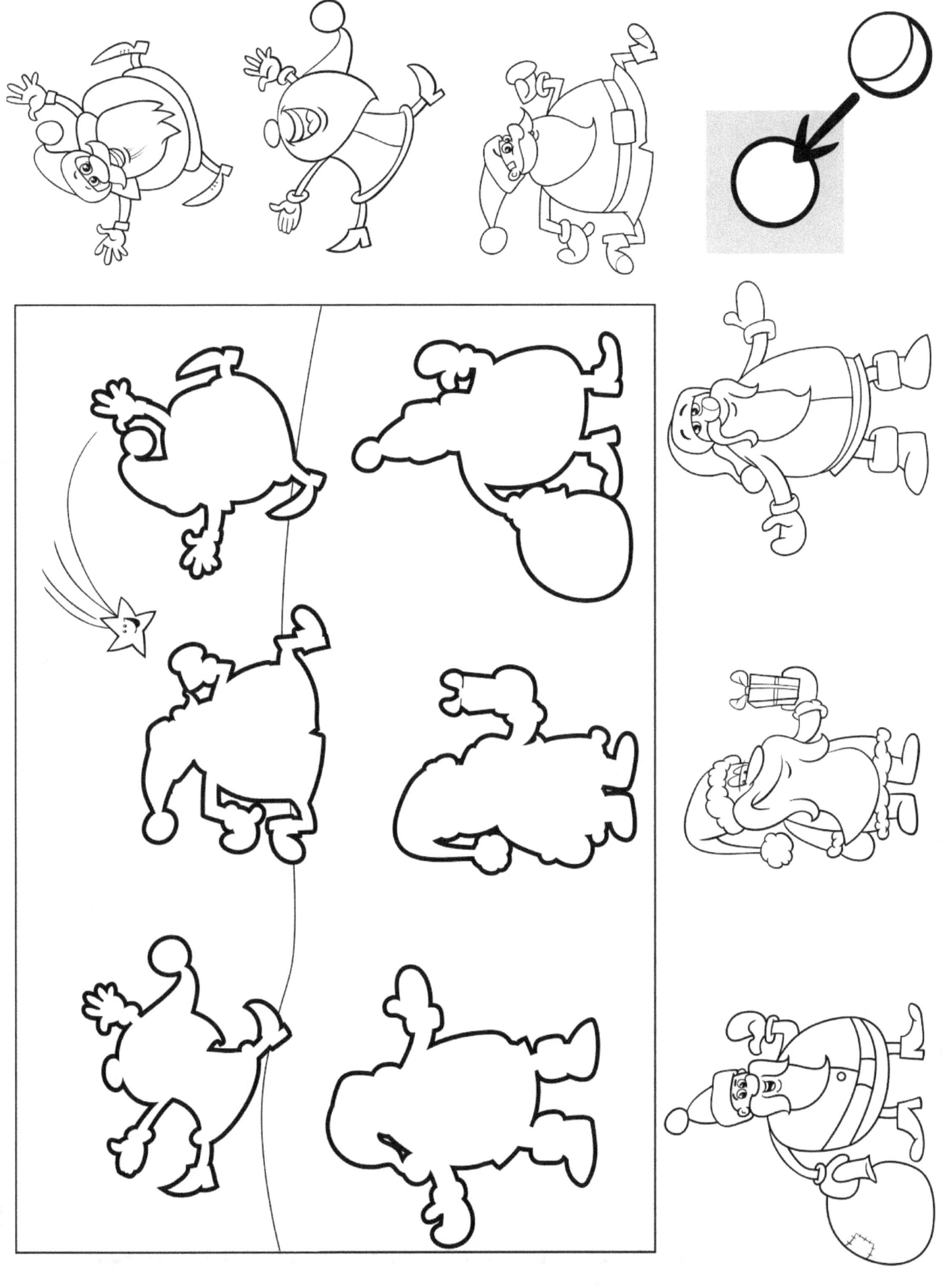

# WHAT COMES NEXT?

ANSWER

1

2

3

4

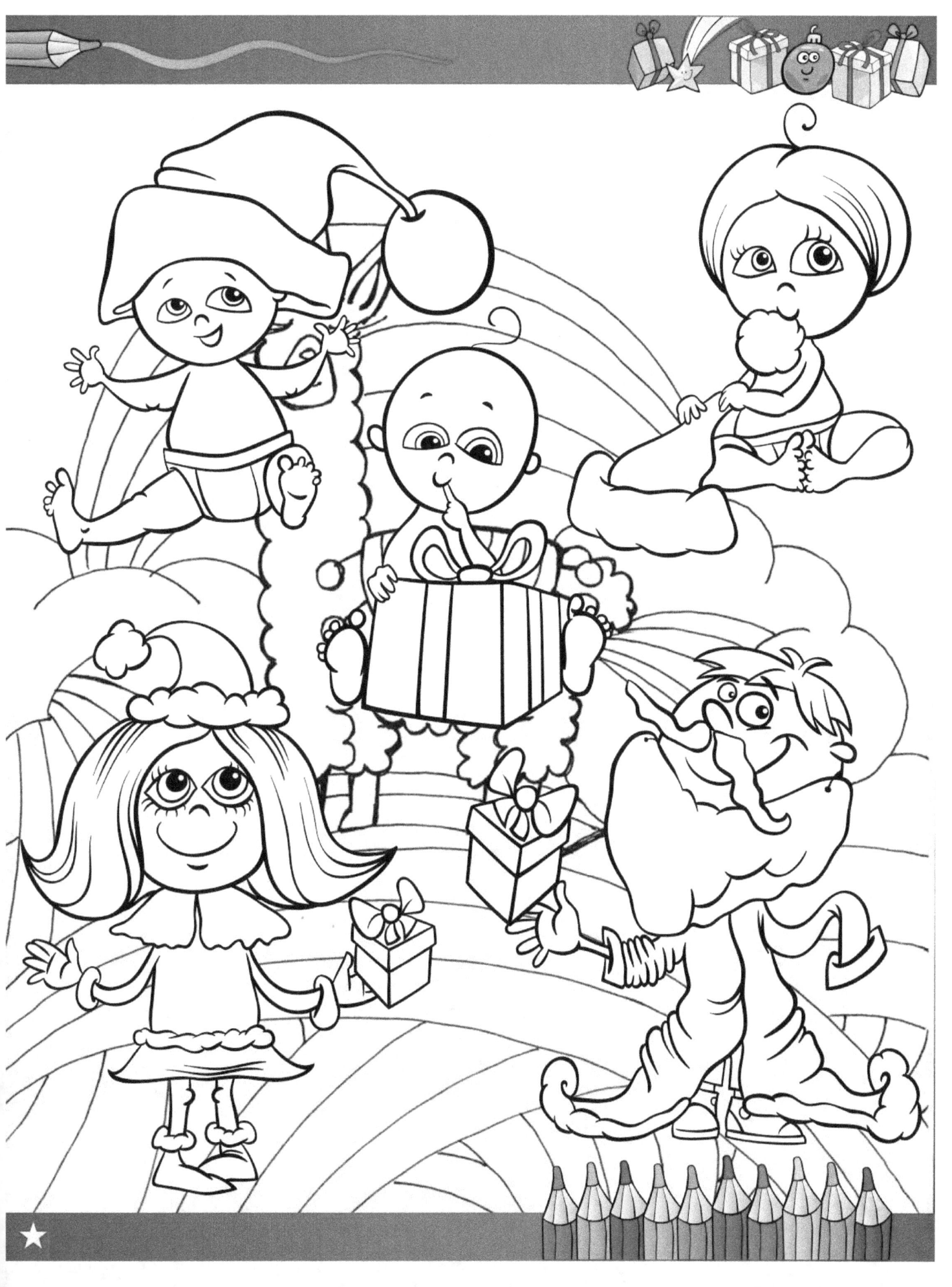

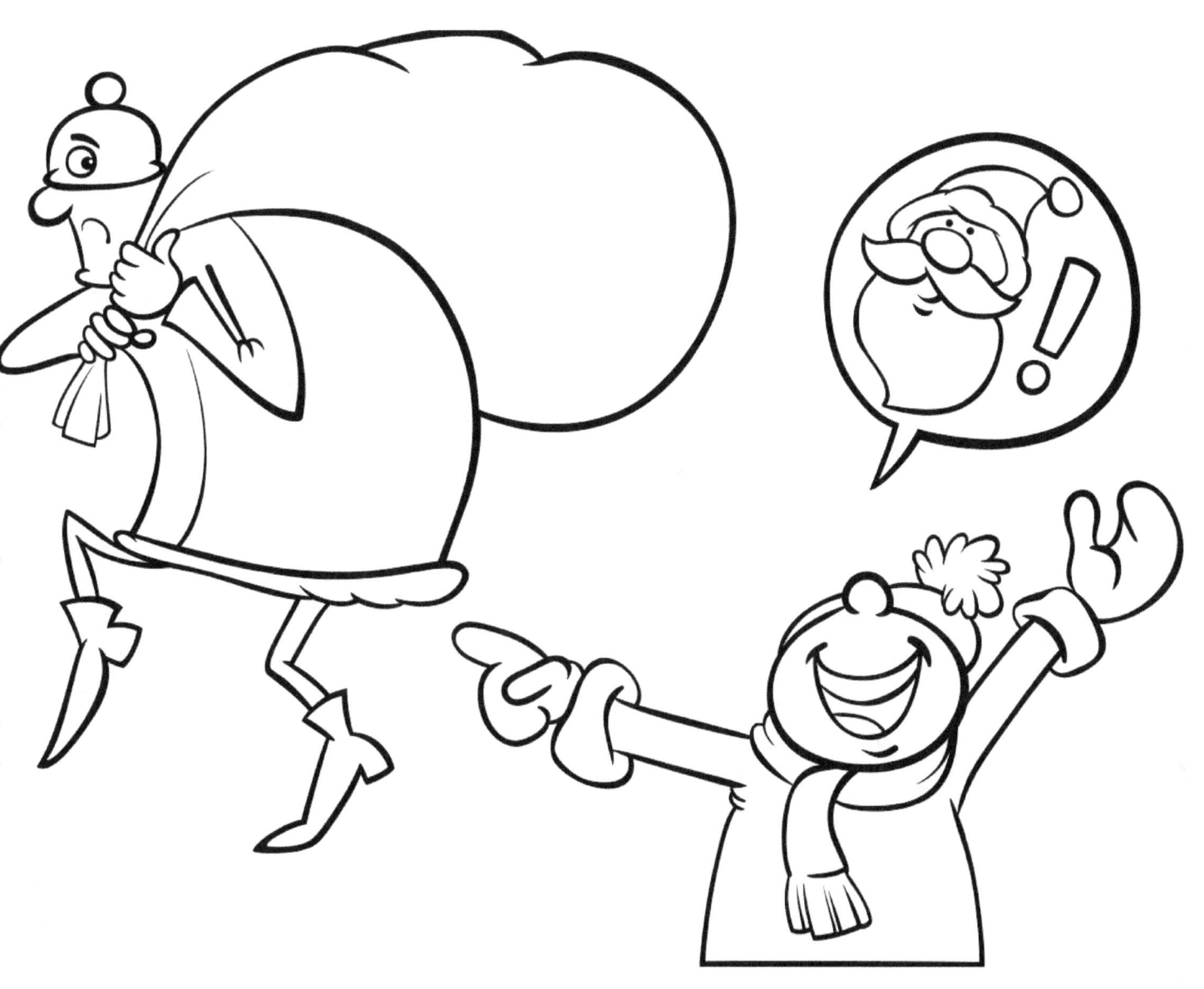

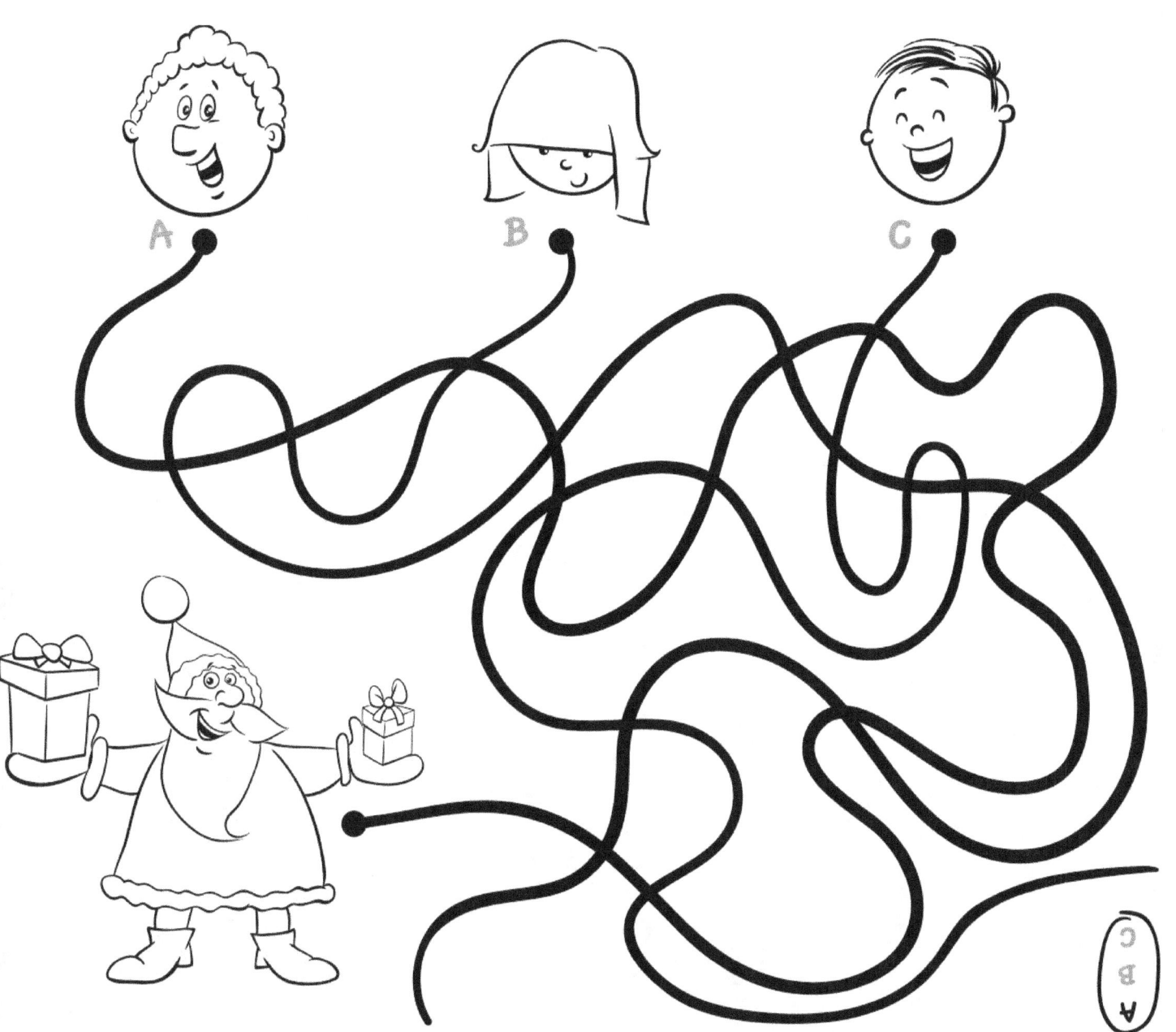

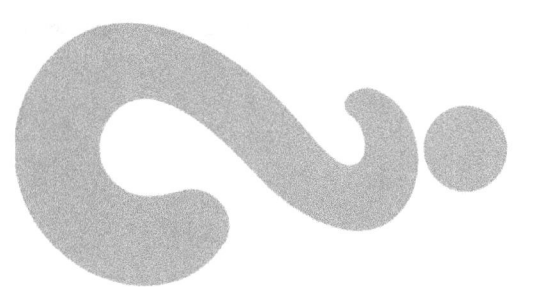

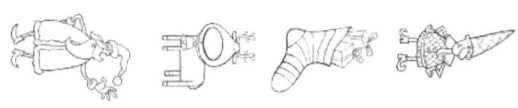

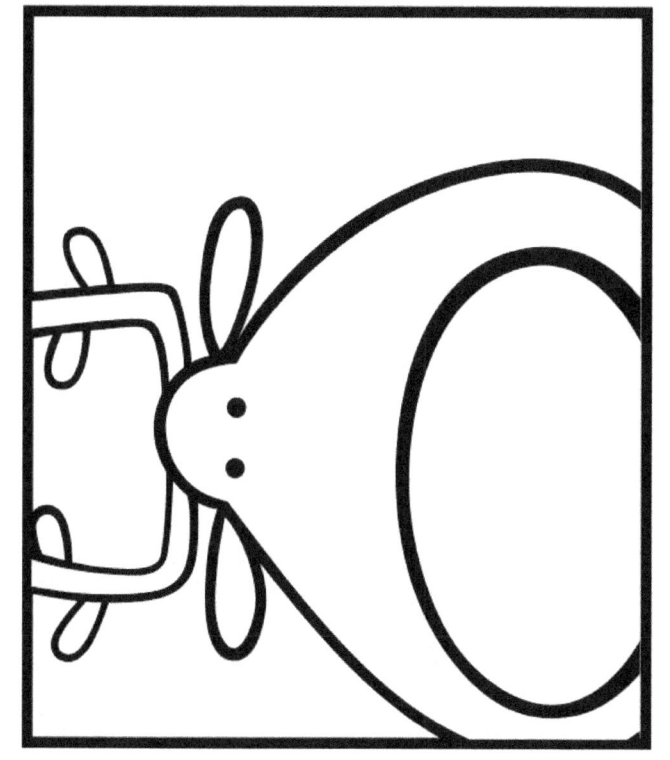

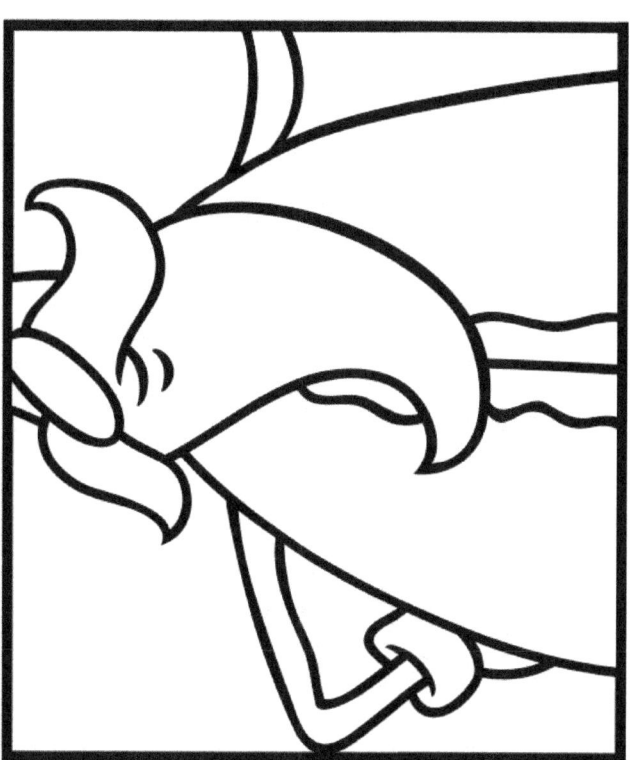

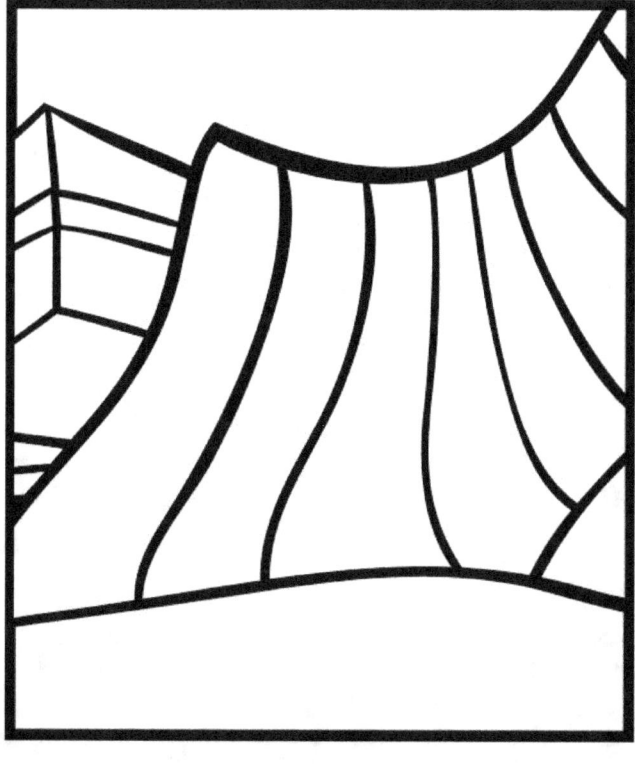

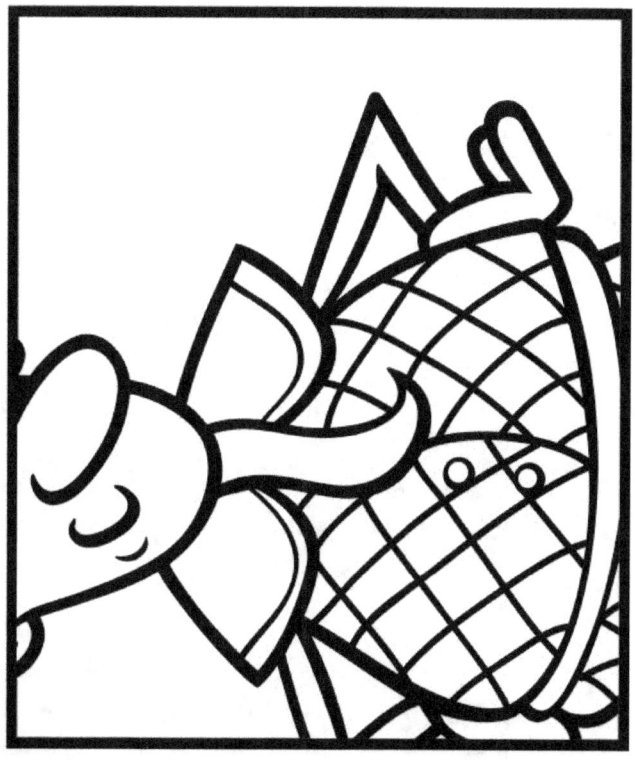

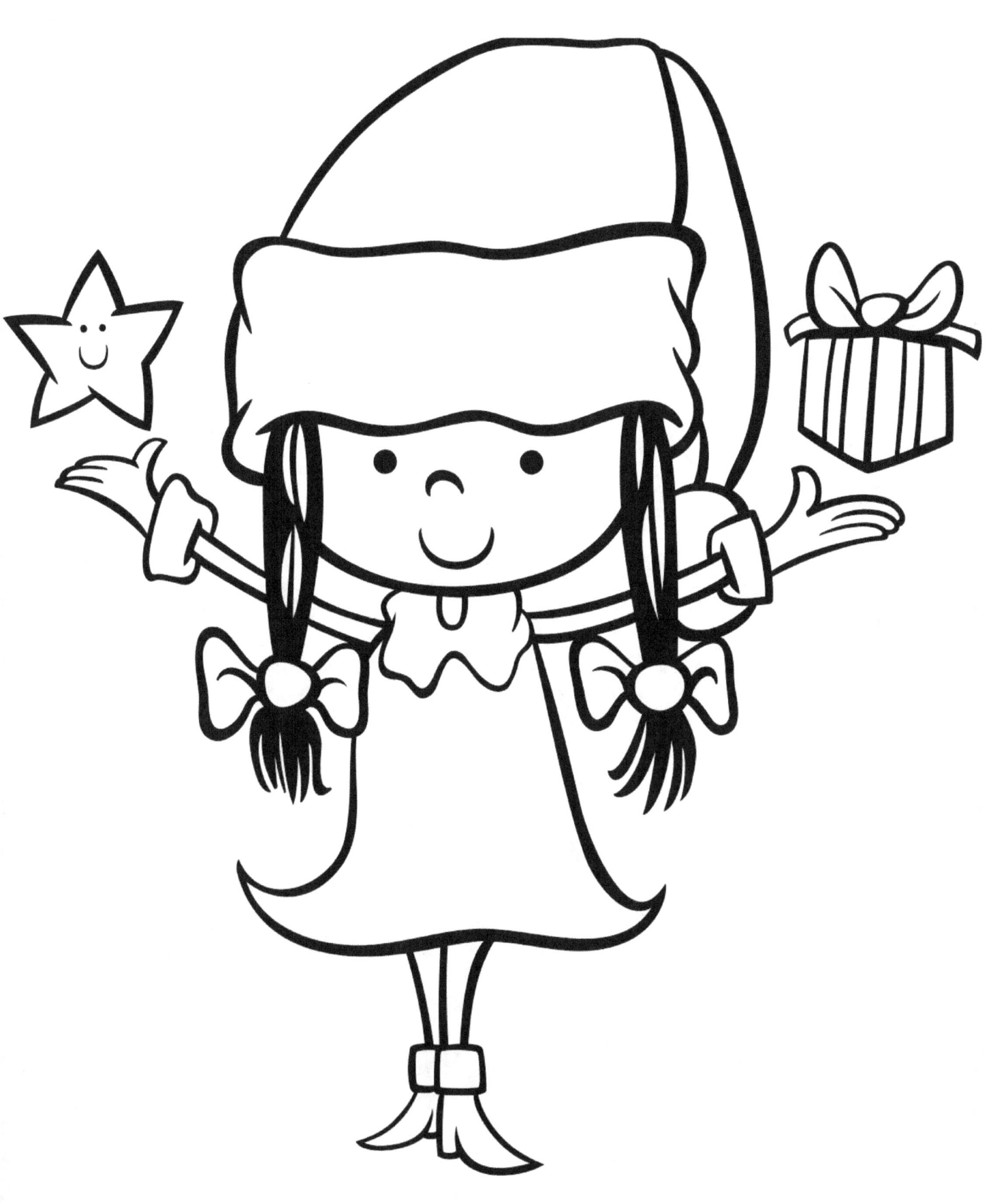

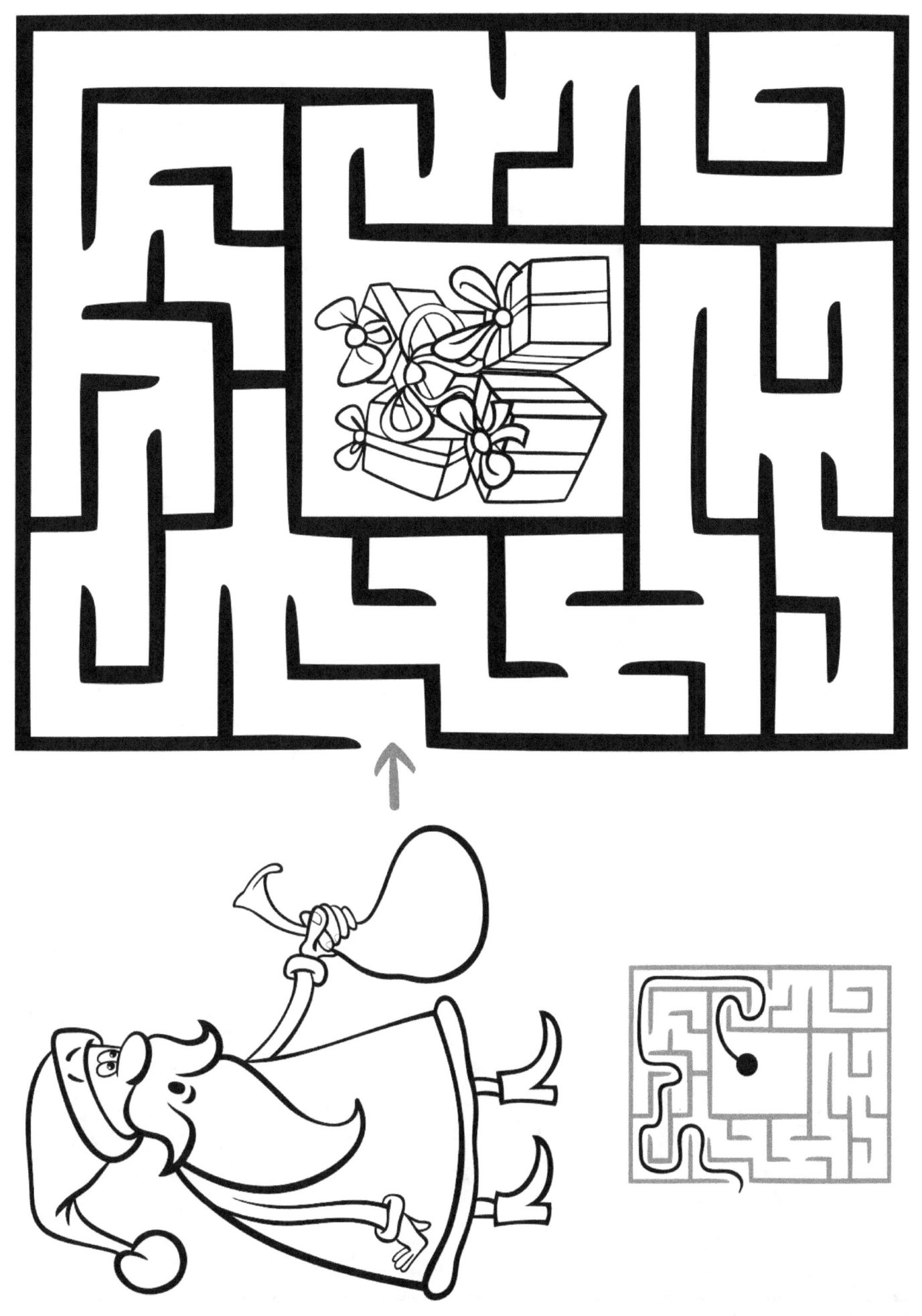

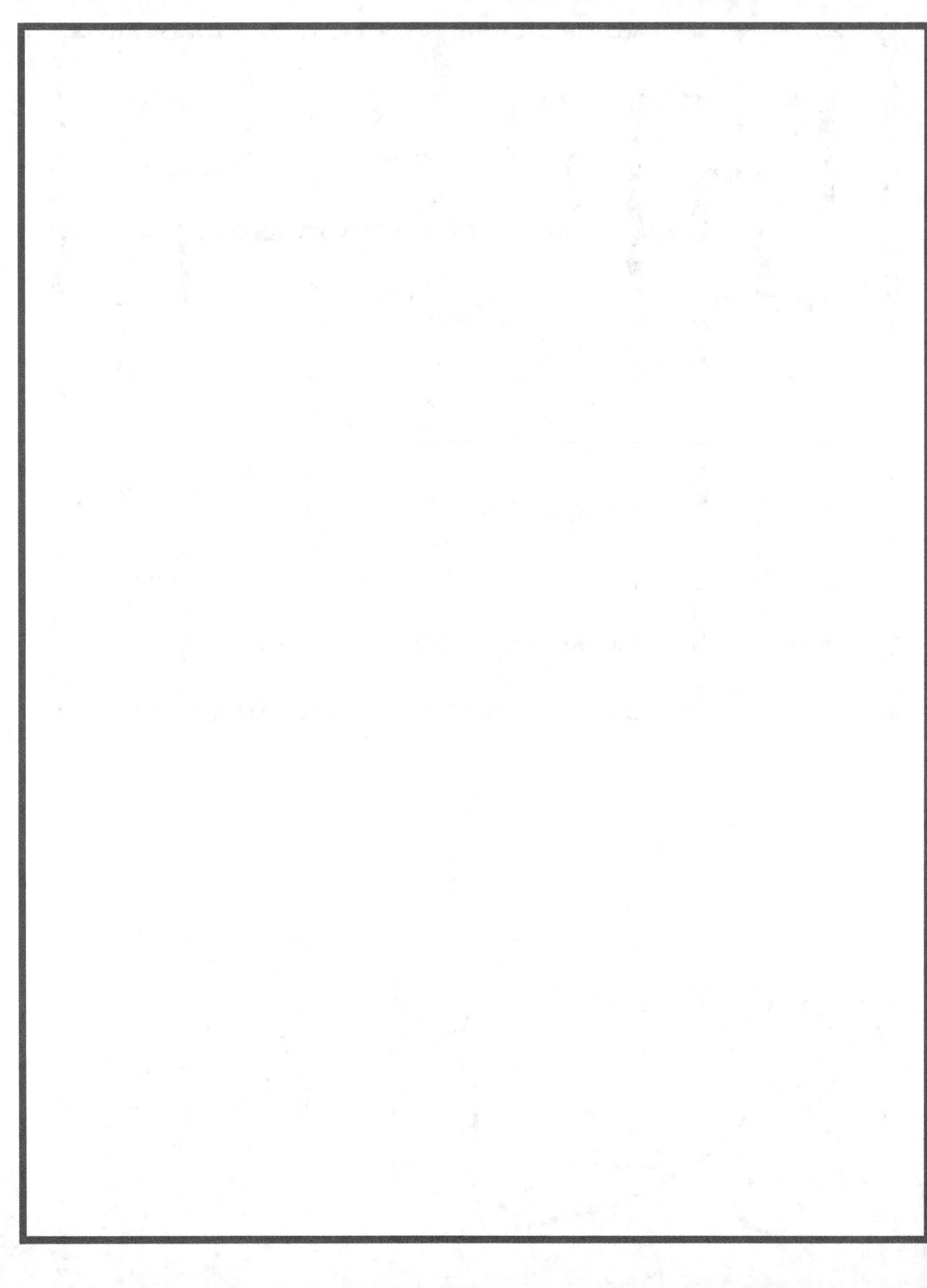

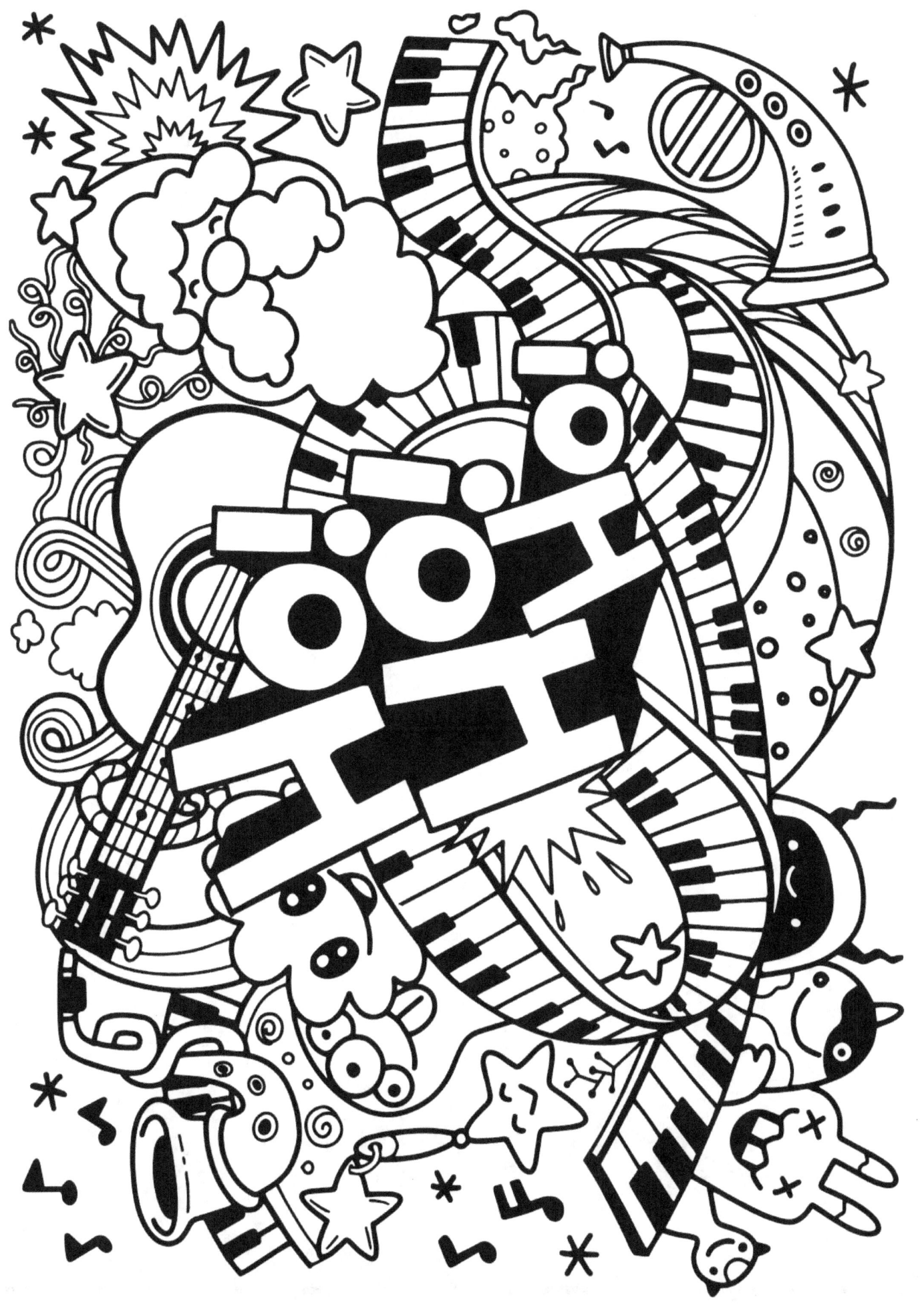

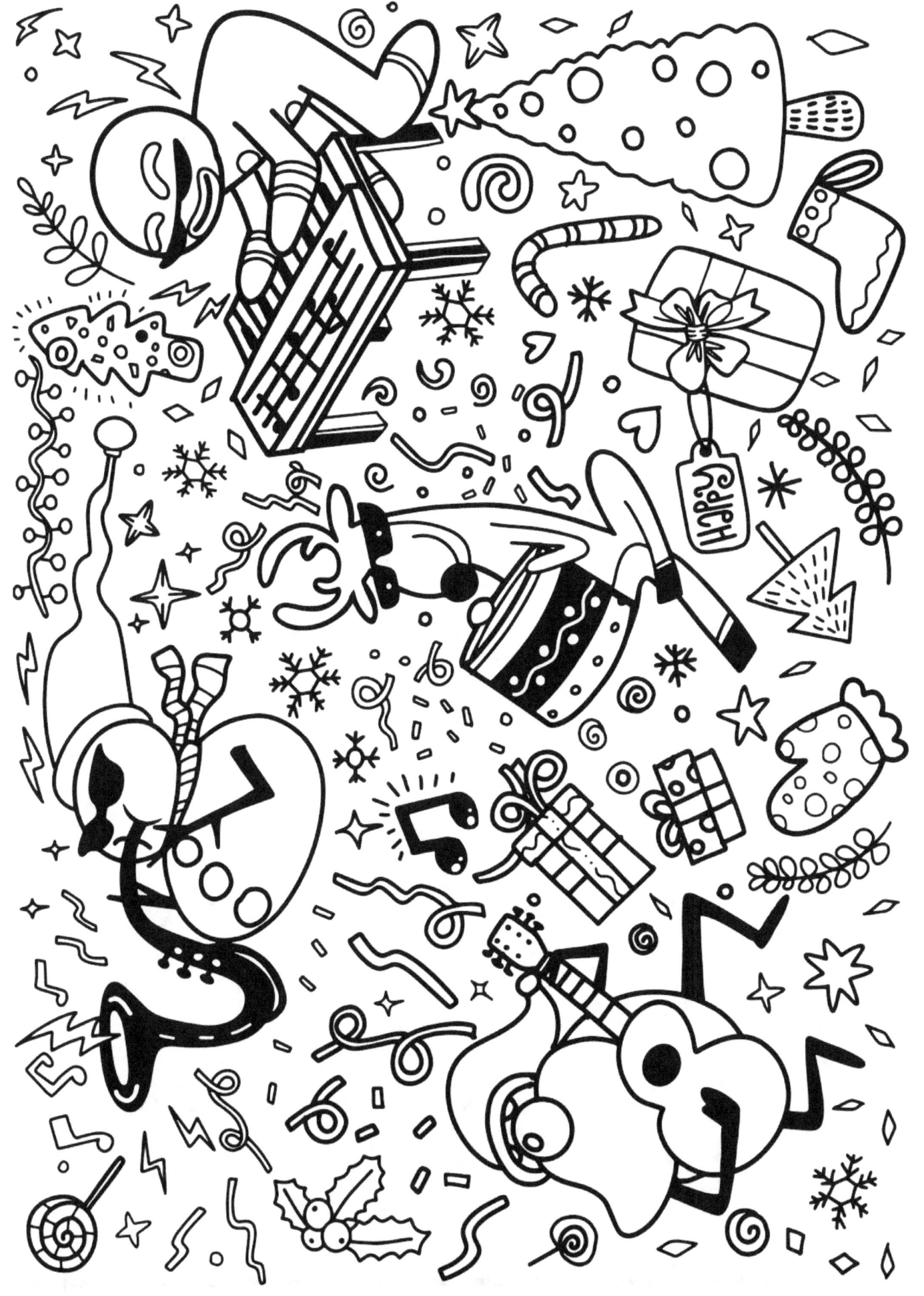

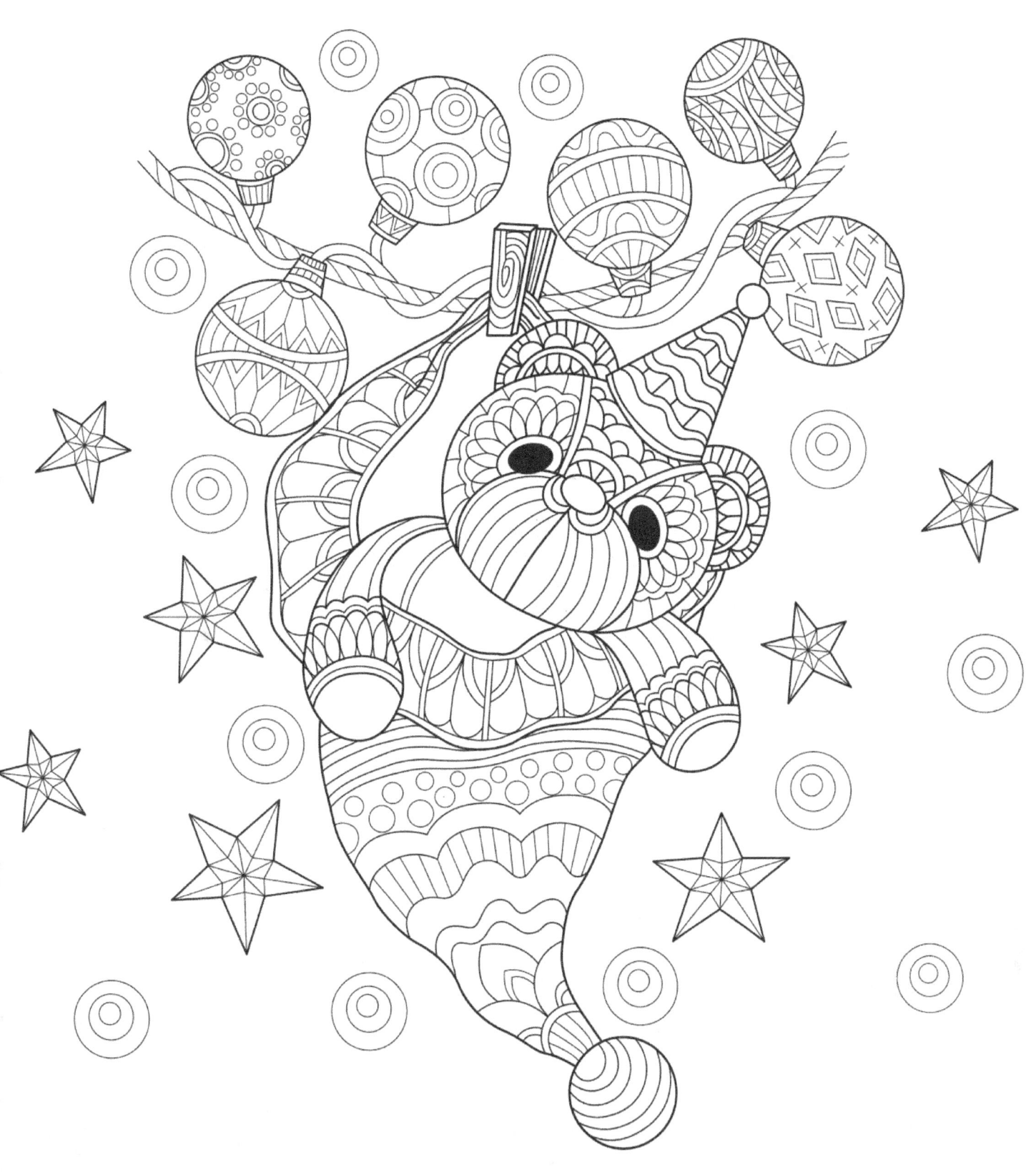

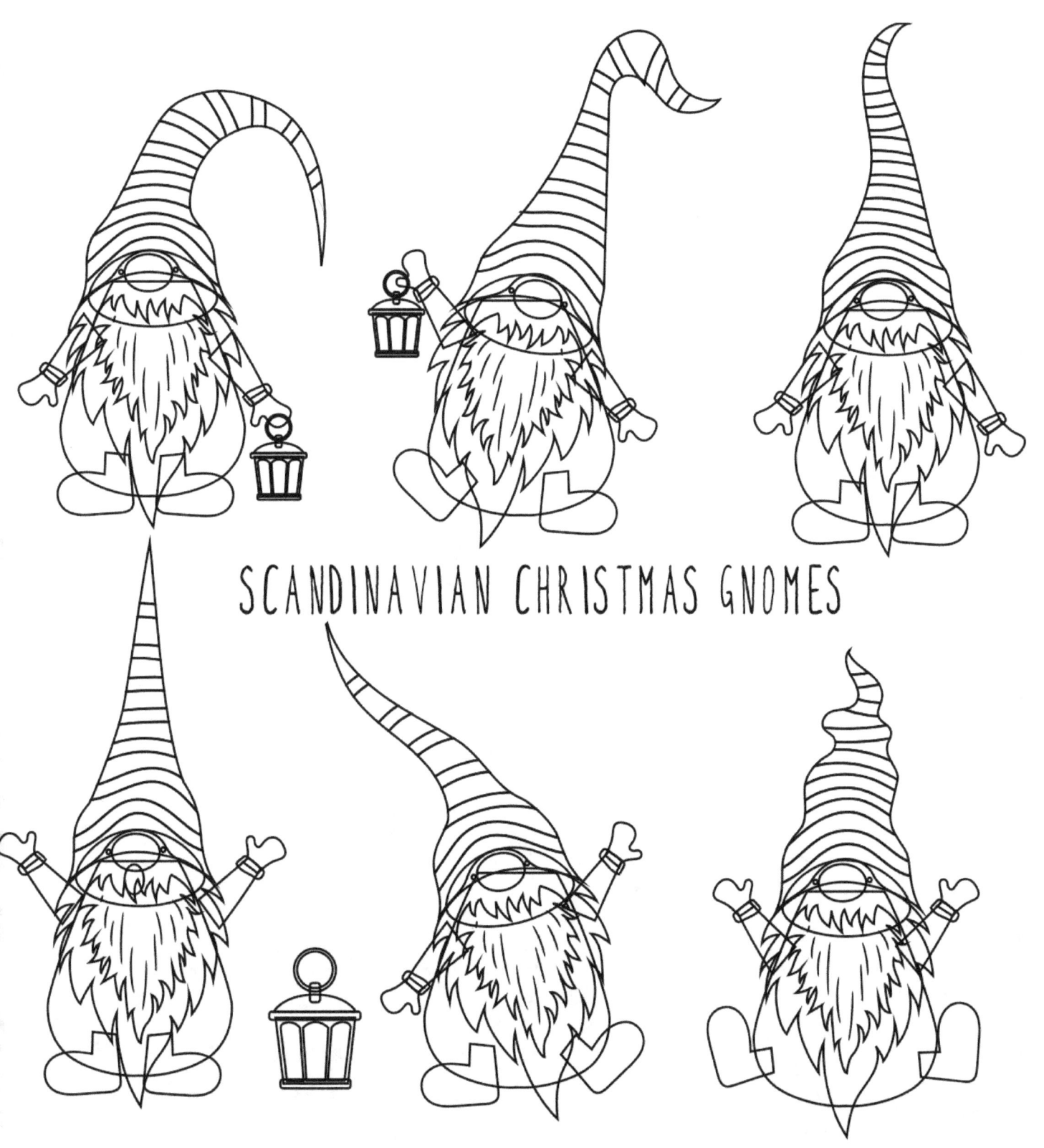

SCANDINAVIAN CHRISTMAS GNOMES

www.ingramcontent.com/pod-product-compliance
Lightning Source LLC
Chambersburg PA
CBHW081543220526
45467CB00010B/3309